# Table of Contents

# Chapter 1: The World of Python and Web Scraping

Welcome to the fascinating realm of web scraping with Python! Whether you're a seasoned programmer or just embarking on your coding journey, this book aims to be your companion through the intricacies and possibilities of extracting data from the web. Let's dive in!

## The Python Phenomenon

Python, named not after the snake, but the British comedy series "Monty Python's Flying Circus," is a language that has captivated the programming world since its inception in the late 1980s by Guido van Rossum. Its design philosophy, "simple is better than complex," makes it an ideal choice for beginners and experts alike.

The rise of Python is a tale of how accessibility, powerful libraries, and community support can propel a language to the forefront of technology. Today, Python is not just a language; it's a tool powering web applications, data analysis, artificial intelligence, and much more.

# Python's Popularity and Applications

Python, a language conceived in the late 1980s, has grown exponentially in popularity over the years. This growth can be attributed to its simplicity, versatility, and the vast ecosystem of libraries and frameworks it supports. Let's delve into the factors behind Python's popularity and its wide-ranging applications.

## Simplicity and Readability

One of Python's core philosophies is simplicity and readability. With a syntax that is clean and easy to understand, Python lowers the barrier to entry for programming. This accessibility makes it an ideal first language for beginners and a powerful tool for experienced developers to quickly prototype and deploy applications.

## Versatile Libraries and Frameworks

Python's extensive libraries and frameworks are a significant factor in its popularity. From web development with Django and Flask to data analysis with Pandas and NumPy, Python's ecosystem is rich and varied. This allows developers to accomplish a wide range of tasks, from building complex web applications to performing sophisticated data analysis.

## Applications in Diverse Fields

Python's applications span multiple industries and disciplines. Here are a few key areas where Python excels:

## 1. Data Science and Machine Learning

Python is a leading language in data science and machine learning. Libraries like Pandas for data manipulation, Matplotlib for data visualization, and TensorFlow and PyTorch for machine learning have made Python an indispensable tool in the data scientist's toolkit.

## 2. Web Development

Python's frameworks such as Django and Flask make web development efficient and scalable. These frameworks support the development of robust web applications, from simple blogs to complex database-driven sites.

## 3. Automation and Scripting

Python is widely used for automating repetitive tasks and scripting. Its simple syntax and powerful standard library make it ideal for writing scripts that automate mundane tasks, saving time and increasing productivity.

## 4. Academic and Scientific Research

Python's simplicity and the availability of scientific libraries like SciPy and NumPy make it a favorite in academic and research communities. It is used for complex scientific calculations, data analysis, and simulation.

## 5. Finance and Trading

In the finance sector, Python is used for quantitative and algorithmic trading, financial analysis, and risk management. Libraries like pandas_datareader and Zipline have enabled Python to play a significant role in financial modeling and trading strategy development.

## 6. Cybersecurity

Python's powerful libraries and its ability to integrate with other languages and systems make it a useful tool in cybersecurity for building security tools, analyzing threats, and automating security processes.

# Python in the Context of Web Scraping

Python's rise as a popular tool for web scraping is no coincidence. Its features, libraries, and community support make it exceptionally well-suited for this task. Let's explore what makes Python a go-to choice for web scraping.

## 1. Ease of Use

Python's straightforward syntax and readability make it an excellent choice for web scraping. These characteristics allow both beginners and experienced developers to easily write scripts that extract data from websites. The simplicity of Python means that more time can be spent on solving the problem at hand rather than deciphering complex code syntax.

## 2. Rich Libraries for Web Scraping

Python boasts a wealth of libraries specifically designed for web scraping and handling HTTP requests. Libraries such as BeautifulSoup, Scrapy, and Selenium provide powerful tools for navigating, selecting, and extracting data from HTML and XML content. These libraries cater to a range of needs – from parsing simple HTML pages to interacting with JavaScript-heavy websites.

- BeautifulSoup: Ideal for beginners, BeautifulSoup is simple to use and powerful enough to extract data from HTML and XML files efficiently.
- Scrapy: An open-source web-crawling framework, Scrapy is designed for scraping and extracting data from websites on a large scale.
- Selenium: While primarily a tool for automating web browsers, Selenium is extremely useful for scraping data from websites that rely heavily on JavaScript.

## 3. Community and Support

Python's large and active community means abundant resources, tutorials, and forums are available for troubleshooting and learning. This support is invaluable, especially when dealing with the unique challenges that web scraping can present.

## 4. Handling Data

Once data is scraped, Python's data manipulation strengths come to the fore. Libraries like Pandas make it easy to clean, analyze, and visualize data, turning raw data scraped from websites into actionable insights.

## 5. Flexibility and Integration

Python allows for seamless integration with other tools and languages, which is crucial in web scraping. You can easily combine Python's scraping capabilities with databases, data analysis tools, and web frameworks, making it a versatile choice for comprehensive web scraping projects.

## 6. Efficient HTTP Handling

Python's `requests` library simplifies the process of making HTTP requests to websites. This is crucial for web scraping, as it allows for easy handling of cookies, sessions, headers, and form data, simulating a real user browsing the web.

Python, with its combination of simplicity, powerful libraries, and a supportive community, is an excellent choice for web scraping. It not only makes the process of extracting data from the web more accessible but also provides the tools to process and analyze this data effectively. As we dive deeper into the specifics of Python web scraping, these strengths will become increasingly apparent, showcasing why Python is a preferred language for web scraping enthusiasts and professionals alike.

# Why Scrape the Web?

In the digital age, where vast amounts of information are available online, web scraping has emerged as a powerful tool for extracting this data. But why go through the trouble of scraping the web? Let's explore the key reasons and the value it brings to different fields.

## 1. Data Availability

The internet is a treasure trove of data. From social media posts to online marketplaces, information is constantly being generated and updated. However, much of this data isn't readily available in a structured format like a spreadsheet or an API. Web scraping allows you to access this vast pool of information, transforming unstructured web data into a structured, usable format.

## 2. Automation and Efficiency

Manual data collection is not only time-consuming but also prone to human error. Web scraping automates this process, enabling you to collect large volumes of data quickly and accurately. This efficiency is invaluable in fields where real-time data analysis is crucial, such as finance and market research.

## 3. Competitive Intelligence

In business, knowledge is power. Companies use web scraping to monitor competitors' websites, tracking changes in pricing, product offerings, and marketing strategies. This intelligence is key to staying competitive in a rapidly evolving marketplace.

## 4. Customized Data Sets

Sometimes, the specific data you need isn't available in pre-packaged formats. Web scraping allows you to tailor your data collection to your specific needs, ensuring you have exactly the data you require for your analysis or project.

## 5. Research and Development

Academics, journalists, and researchers rely on web scraping to gather data for studies, reports, and investigations. The ability to quickly collect and analyze data from various sources can lead to new insights and breakthroughs in various fields.

## 6. SEO and Digital Marketing

In SEO and digital marketing, understanding the online landscape is crucial. Web scraping helps in tracking keyword rankings, understanding audience preferences, and monitoring backlinks, contributing significantly to developing effective strategies.

## 7. Legal Compliance

For legal professionals, staying updated with the latest regulations, case laws, and legal precedents is essential. Web scraping can automate the monitoring of legal websites and government portals, ensuring quick access to important legal updates.

## 8. E-commerce and Price Monitoring

For e-commerce businesses, keeping tabs on market trends, customer reviews, and pricing strategies is vital. Web scraping enables these businesses to gather this data efficiently, helping them make informed decisions about pricing, inventory, and marketing strategies.

## Decoding Web Scraping

Web scraping is the art and science of extracting data from websites. It is a technique that has evolved with the internet, growing from simple text extraction to handling dynamic websites powered by JavaScript. In this digital age, where data is the new gold, web scraping has become an essential skill for data analysts, marketers, and developers.

Understanding the legal and ethical implications of web scraping is crucial. While the internet is a treasure trove of data, it's important to scrape responsibly, respecting both the law and website terms of service.

## The Power of Python in Web Scraping

Python's simplicity and the richness of its libraries make it an excellent choice for web scraping. Libraries like BeautifulSoup, Scrapy, and Selenium have made Python synonymous with web scraping. These tools not only simplify the extraction process but also handle complexities like session management, data parsing, and more.

# Getting Started with Python and Web Scraping

Before diving into the exciting world of web scraping, you'll need to set up your development environment. This involves installing Python, creating a virtual environment, and installing the required libraries. Let's walk through these steps for Windows, Mac, and Linux systems.

## Installing Python

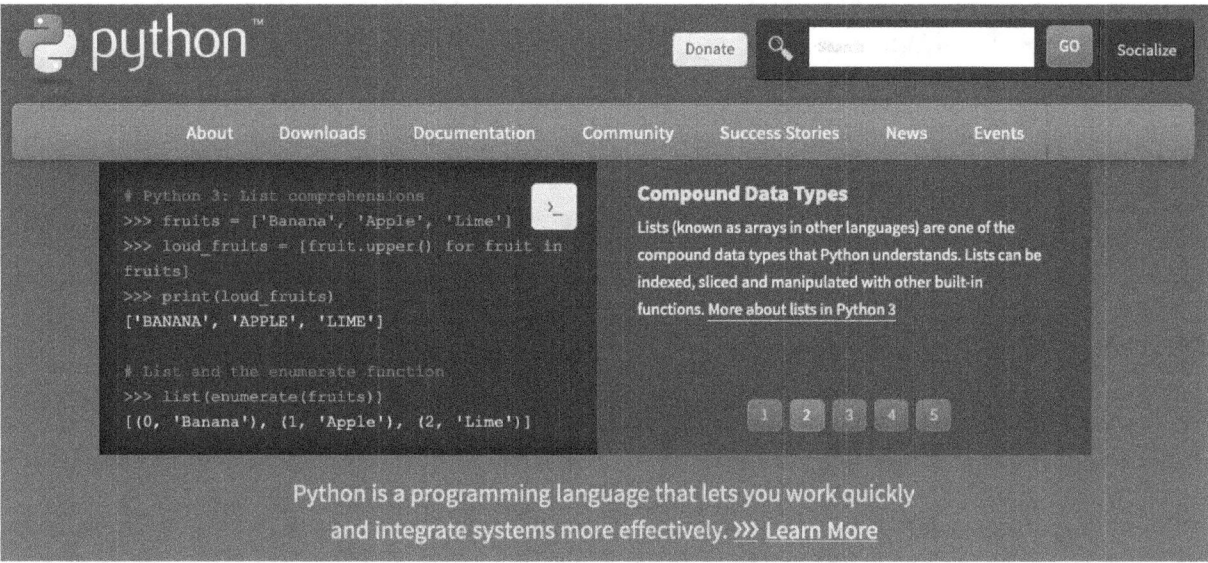

### Windows:

1. Download the Python installer from python.org.
2. Run the installer. Ensure you check the box that says "Add Python to PATH" before clicking "Install Now."

### Mac:

1. Python often comes pre-installed on Mac. To check, open Terminal and type `python --version`. If it's not installed or you need a different version, use Homebrew to install
2. Download Homebrew
3. Install Homebrew

```
brew install python3
```

### Linux:

1. Most Linux distributions come with Python pre-installed. You can check by opening a terminal and typing `python --version`.

2. If you need to install or update Python, use your distribution's package manager. For example, on Ubuntu, you can run `sudo apt-get install python3`.

## Setting Up a Virtual Environment

A virtual environment is a self-contained directory that contains a Python installation for a particular version of Python, plus a number of additional packages.

1. Open your command line interface (Terminal on Mac and Linux, Command Prompt or PowerShell on Windows).
2. Navigate to the directory where you want to create your project.
3. Run `python -m venv myenv` (replace `myenv` with your desired environment name). This creates a new virtual environment.
4. Activate the environment:
   - **Windows:** `myenv\Scripts\activate`
   - **Mac/Linux:** `source myenv/bin/activate`

## Installing Required Libraries

With your virtual environment activated, you can now install BeautifulSoup and Requests, which are needed for the web scraping example.

1. Ensure your virtual environment is active. You should see the environment name (`myenv`) in your command line prompt.
2. Install BeautifulSoup and Requests by running:

```
pip install beautifulsoup4 requests
```

## Running the Example

Now that you've set up Python, created a virtual environment, and installed the necessary libraries, you're ready to run the web scraping example.

1. Create a new Python file in your project directory (e.g., `scrape_example.py`).
2. Copy the BeautifulSoup example code into this file.
3. Save the file and run it using:

```
python scrape_example.py
```

And that's it! You've successfully run your first web scraping script. As you continue through this book, you'll learn more about Python, web scraping, and how to leverage these skills to extract valuable data from the web.

# Practical Example: A Glimpse into BeautifulSoup

Let's look at a practical example using BeautifulSoup, a popular Python library for parsing HTML and XML documents. This simple script demonstrates how you can extract titles from a webpage:

```python
from bs4 import BeautifulSoup
import requests

# Fetch the content from a webpage
url = "https:// https://www.opensourceshakespeare.org/views/plays/plays.php"
response = requests.get(url)
soup = BeautifulSoup(response.text, 'html.parser')

# Extract and print each title
for title in soup.find_all('strong'):
    print(title.get_text())
```

```
> python3 main.py
SEARCH TEXTS
Plays
                                    Sonnets
                                    Poems
                                    Concordance
                                    Advanced Search
                                    About OSS

COMEDIES
All's Well That Ends Well
As You Like It
Comedy of Errors
Love's Labour's Lost
Measure for Measure
Merchant of Venice
Merry Wives of Windsor
Midsummer Night's Dream
Much Ado about Nothing
Taming of the Shrew
Tempest
Twelfth Night
Two Gentlemen of Verona
Winter's Tale
HISTORIES
Henry IV, Part I
Henry IV, Part II
Henry V
Henry VI, Part I
Henry VI, Part II
Henry VI, Part III
Henry VIII
King John
Pericles
Richard II
Richard III
```

```
TRAGEDIES
Antony and Cleopatra
Coriolanus
Cymbeline
Hamlet
Julius Caesar
King Lear
Macbeth
Othello
Romeo and Juliet
Timon of Athens
Titus Andronicus
Troilus and Cressida
```

This snippet is just a teaser of what's possible. As we progress through this book, you'll learn how to navigate and extract data from complex websites, handle different data formats, and much more.

# Chapter 2: Python Essentials for Web Scraping

## Objective of Chapter 2

In this chapter, we aim to lay the groundwork for your journey into web scraping with Python. We'll cover the essential Python concepts and skills you'll need to confidently navigate and extract data from the web. Whether you're new to Python or looking to brush up your skills, this chapter will provide you with the necessary foundation for effective web scraping.

## Introduction to Python Essentials for Web Scraping

Welcome to Chapter 2! As we embark on this journey, it's crucial to understand that web scraping is more than just running scripts to extract data; it's about understanding the tools and language you're working with. Python, with its simplicity and power, is our chosen tool for this adventure.

In this chapter, we will delve into the core aspects of Python that are particularly relevant to web scraping. We'll start with the basic syntax and structure of Python programming, ensuring you're comfortable with the language's fundamentals. From there, we'll explore Python's handling of strings, lists, and dictionaries, which are essential when manipulating scraped data.

Next, we'll touch on error handling and debugging in Python, skills that are invaluable when your scraping scripts encounter the unexpected. We'll also introduce you to working with files in Python, as storing and retrieving the data you scrape is a key part of the process.

Lastly, we'll take a brief look at Python's `requests` library and how it can be used to make HTTP requests. This is a fundamental skill in web scraping, as it's the initial step in retrieving data from the web.

By the end of this chapter, you will have a solid understanding of Python basics and be well-prepared to tackle more complex web scraping tasks in the upcoming chapters. So, let's get started and dive into the world of Python programming!

## Chapter 2: Understanding Variables in Python

In the world of programming, variables are like the building blocks of your code. They are containers that hold data, allowing you to store and manipulate information within your Python programs. To put it simply, variables are how we give names to data.

Imagine you're working on a project, and you need to store the age of your pet, Fluffy the cat. You could use a variable like this:

```
fluffy_age = 5
```

In this example, `fluffy_age` is the variable name, and 5 is the data it holds, which is Fluffy's age. This concept might seem straightforward, but there's more to variables in Python than meets the eye.

**Variable Naming Rules:** Python has some rules for naming variables:

- Variable names can only contain letters, numbers, and underscores.
- They cannot start with a number.
- Variable names are case-sensitive, so `fluffy_age` and `Fluffy_Age` would be considered different variables.

**Data Types:** Variables can store different types of data. Here are some common data types you'll encounter:

- **int**: Used for integers (whole numbers), e.g., `age = 25`.
- **float**: Used for floating-point numbers (decimal numbers), e.g., `pi = 3.14159`.
- **str**: Used for strings (text), e.g., `name = "John"`.
- **bool**: Used for Boolean values (True or False), e.g., `is_happy = True`.

**Assigning Values:** You assign values to variables using the = operator. For example, to assign the value 42 to a variable called `answer`, you would write `answer = 42`.

**Changing Variable Values:** Variables are not set in stone. You can change their values by reassigning them:

```
fluffy_age = 6   # Fluffy had a birthday!
```

**Why Use Variables?** Variables make your code readable and maintainable. Instead of using raw data throughout your program, you give data meaningful names. This helps you and other developers understand your code more easily.

Here's a quick recap: variables are like containers for your data, they have rules for naming, can store different types of data, and you can change their values as needed.

In the world of Python web scraping, understanding how to use variables is just the beginning. Soon, you'll be using them to store URLs, HTML content, and all sorts of data as you embark on your web scraping journey. So, keep these basics in mind, and let's move forward in your Python web scraping adventure!

### The Significance of Booleans: Making Decisions with True and False

In our exploration of variables, we've covered integers, floats, and strings, but there's one more essential data type we shouldn't overlook - Booleans. While they may seem simple, Booleans are the backbone of decision-making in Python and programming as a whole.

## What Are Booleans?

Booleans are named after the great mathematician and logician George Boole. In Python, a Boolean can only have one of two values: True or False. They represent binary choices, like yes or no, on or off, and are fundamental to control flow in programming.

## The Power of True and False

Booleans are the secret sauce behind conditional statements, which we explored earlier in this chapter. When you want your program to make decisions, Booleans come to the rescue. Here's why they're essential:

**1. Decision Making:** Conditional statements like "if" and "while" rely on Boolean expressions. They check whether a condition is True or False to determine which code path to follow. For example, you might use a Boolean variable called `is_raining` to decide whether to bring an umbrella.

**2. Loop Control:** Booleans play a crucial role in controlling loops. You can use them to decide when to exit a loop with a "break" statement or skip specific iterations with a "continue" statement.

**3. Error Handling:** In error handling and exception handling, Booleans help you identify whether an error condition exists and take appropriate actions.

**4. State Tracking:** Booleans are often used to track the state of a program. For instance, you might use a Boolean variable called `logged_in` to check if a user is currently signed in.

## Practical Applications

Booleans are everywhere in programming, from building user interfaces to data analysis and web scraping. Here are a few practical examples of how Booleans are used:

- **User Authentication:** When a user logs in, a Boolean variable is often set to True to indicate that the user is authenticated.
- **Web Scraping:** Booleans can be used to check if a certain element is present on a web page, helping your scraper make decisions based on page content.
- **Game Development:** In game development, Booleans can be used to track game states, such as whether a level is completed or a character is alive.
- **Data Filtering:** Booleans are crucial for filtering and analyzing data. You can use them to create conditions for data selection or transformation.

# Mastering Control Flow with "if" and "else" Clauses

Now that we've got a grip on variables, it's time to dive into one of the fundamental building blocks of programming logic - conditional statements. In Python, these are primarily expressed through the "if" and "else" clauses.

## The Power of Conditional Statements

Conditional statements allow your program to make decisions. Think of them as the logic that guides your program's behavior. Imagine you're building a weather app, and you want it to tell users whether to bring an umbrella or not. Conditional statements are your go-to tool for this task.

## The "if" Statement

Let's start with the "if" statement. It begins with the word "if," followed by a condition in parentheses and a colon. If that condition evaluates to True, the code inside the "if" block runs. If it's False, the code inside the "if" block is skipped.

```
weather = "rainy"
if weather == "rainy":
    print("Don't forget your umbrella!")
```

In this example, the condition `weather == "rainy"` checks if the `weather` variable holds the value "rainy." If it does, the message is printed.

## The "else" Clause

What if you want to provide an alternative action when the condition is not met? Enter the "else" clause. Here's how it works:

```
weather = "sunny"
if weather == "rainy":
    print("Don't forget your umbrella!")
else:
    print("Enjoy the sunshine!")
```

In this case, if the `weather` is not "rainy," the code inside the "else" block executes. It's like having a plan B for your program.

## Combining Conditions with "elif"

Often, you need to check multiple conditions. That's where "elif" (short for "else if") comes in. You can chain multiple "if" and "elif" statements together to create more complex decision trees.

```
temperature = 25
if temperature < 10:
    print("It's freezing!")
```

```
elif temperature < 20:
    print("It's chilly.")
else:
    print("It's a beautiful day!")
```

In this example, we check the temperature and print a message based on different ranges.

## Logical Operators

To create more sophisticated conditions, you can use logical operators like "and" and "or" to combine multiple conditions.

```
is_raining = True
has_umbrella = False
if is_raining and not has_umbrella:
    print("Get ready to get wet!")
```

Here, we check if it's raining and the person doesn't have an umbrella, then we print a message.

## Indentation Matters

In Python, indentation is crucial. Unlike other languages that use braces or keywords, Python uses indentation to determine the scope of code blocks. Be consistent with your indentation, using spaces or tabs, but not both.

## Practice Makes Perfect

Learning "if" and "else" statements takes practice. Start with simple conditions and gradually work your way up to more complex logic. Experiment with different scenarios and see how your program responds.

## Sum it all up

Conditional statements are a vital tool in your programming toolkit. They allow your code to make decisions, adapt to different situations, and provide dynamic user experiences. As you continue your journey into Python web scraping, you'll find these clauses invaluable for handling various scenarios and making your code more intelligent.

So, embrace the power of "if" and "else," and let your Python programs make decisions that enhance their functionality and utility.

Embracing the Power of Loops - "while" and "for" in Python

In our journey through Python, we've conquered variables and mastered conditional statements. Now, it's time to take the next step and learn about loops. Loops are like your trusty sidekicks, tirelessly performing repetitive tasks so you don't have to.

## The "while" Loop

Let's start with the "while" loop. This loop keeps running a block of code as long as a certain condition is true. It's like telling your code, "Keep doing this until I say stop." Here's how it works:

```python
count = 0
while count < 5:
    print(f"Count: {count}")
    count += 1
```

In this example, the loop keeps printing the value of count as long as it's less than 5. Once count reaches 5, the loop stops.

## The "for" Loop

The "for" loop, on the other hand, is your go-to tool when you want to iterate over a sequence (like a list, tuple, or string) or any iterable. It's like telling your code, "Go through this collection and do something with each item."

```python
fruits = ["apple", "banana", "cherry"]
for fruit in fruits:
    print(f"I love {fruit}s!")
```

In this example, the "for" loop goes through the list of fruits and prints a message for each one.

## Loop Control Statements

Loops come with some handy control statements to modify their behavior. Here are two important ones:

- **"break"** - This statement allows you to exit the loop prematurely if a certain condition is met. It's like saying, "I'm done here; let's move on."

```python
for number in range(1, 11):
    if number == 5:
        break
    print(number)
```

In this case, the loop breaks when number equals 5.

- **"continue"** - Use this statement to skip the rest of the current iteration and move on to the next one. It's like saying, "Skip this one; let's see what's next."

```python
for number in range(1, 6):
    if number == 3:
        continue
    print(number)
```

In this example, the loop skips printing the number 3 and continues with the next iteration.

## Infinite Loops

Be cautious with loops; they can lead to infinite loops if not used carefully. An infinite loop runs forever, which can crash your program. Always ensure your loop's condition eventually becomes false to avoid this.

## Practice, Practice, Practice

As with anything in programming, practice is key. Start with simple loops and gradually tackle more complex tasks. Experiment with "while" and "for" loops, use control statements to fine-tune your loops, and explore various scenarios.

## Sum it all up

Loops are your allies in automating repetitive tasks and processing data efficiently. Whether it's reading files, scraping web pages, or crunching numbers, loops are the tools that make it all possible. As you continue your Python web scraping journey, remember the power of loops and how they can save you time and effort.

So, embrace the elegance of "while" and "for" loops, and let them be your companions in tackling tasks big and small.

## Comments in Python

Comments in Python are a way to include explanatory notes or remarks within your code. Comments are not executed by the Python interpreter; they exist solely for the benefit of the programmers and anyone else who might read the code. They are incredibly valuable for documenting your code, providing context, and making it more understandable.

Here's how you create comments in Python and how they are commonly used:

## Syntax for Comments

In Python, you can create comments using the # symbol. Anything after # on a line is considered a comment and is ignored by the Python interpreter. For example:

```python
# This is a comment
```

# Purpose of Comments

1. **Explanatory Notes**: Comments can be used to explain the purpose of a variable, function, or block of code. This helps other programmers (including your future self) understand what the code does.

```
# Calculate the total cost
total_cost = quantity * price
```

**Documentation**: Comments can be used to document your code, providing details about how it works, what it expects as input, and what it produces as output. This is especially important for functions and complex algorithms.

```
def calculate_average(numbers):
    """
    Calculate the average of a list of numbers.

    Args:
        numbers (list): A list of numbers.

    Returns:
        float: The average of the numbers.
    """
    total = sum(numbers)
    return total / len(numbers)
```

**Disable Code**: You can temporarily disable a line or block of code by commenting it out. This is useful when debugging or testing different parts of your code.

```
# print("This line is commented out")
```

**TODOs and Reminders**: Comments can be used to leave notes for yourself or your team about tasks that need to be completed or issues that need to be addressed in the future.

```
# TODO: Implement error handling here
```

**Clarify Complex Code**: When you're dealing with complex algorithms or tricky logic, comments can help break down the steps and provide insights into the code's inner workings.

```
# Step 1: Initialize variables
# Step 2: Perform calculations
# Step 3: Return the result
```

# Best Practices

- **Be Descriptive**: Write comments that provide meaningful information. Avoid overly obvious comments like x = x + 1, which don't add any value.

- **Keep Comments Updated**: If you make changes to your code, remember to update the comments to reflect those changes. Outdated comments can be misleading.
- **Follow a Consistent Style**: Choose a consistent style for your comments, such as using sentence case or writing them in the imperative form.
- **Use Docstrings for Functions**: For functions, consider using docstrings (triple-quoted strings) to provide detailed documentation. These can be accessed using the `help()` function.
- **Avoid Overcommenting**: While comments are essential, don't overdo it. Code should be self-explanatory whenever possible, and comments should complement, not replace, clear code.

In summary, comments in Python are a valuable tool for enhancing code readability, providing context, and documenting your programs. Use them wisely to make your code more understandable and maintainable for yourself and others who may work with it.

Mastering Python's List Comprehension

In our journey through Python's versatile toolset, we've tackled variables, conditional statements, and loops. Now, it's time to supercharge your Python programming skills with a feature that's as elegant as it is powerful: list comprehension.

## What is List Comprehension?

List comprehension is a concise and expressive way to create lists in Python. It allows you to build a new list by applying an expression to each item in an existing iterable (like a list, tuple, or range) and optionally filtering those items based on a condition. It's a powerful alternative to traditional for loops for creating lists.

Here's the basic syntax of list comprehension:

```
new_list = [expression for item in iterable if condition]
```

- `expression`: This is the operation or transformation you want to apply to each item from the iterable.
- `item`: Represents each element in the iterable.
- `iterable`: The source of data you're iterating over.
- `condition` (optional): An expression that filters the items. Only items that satisfy this condition are included in the new list.

## The Beauty of List Comprehension

List comprehension shines for several reasons:

**1. Conciseness:** With list comprehension, you can achieve in a single line what might take several lines of code with a traditional for loop. This leads to more readable and compact code.

**2. Readability:** List comprehensions are highly readable because they express the intent of your code in a clear and concise manner. This is especially valuable when working with data transformations.

**3. Efficiency:** List comprehensions are often faster than equivalent for loops, as they're optimized internally by Python.

## Examples of List Comprehension

Let's dive into some practical examples:

### Example 1: Squaring Numbers

Suppose you have a list of numbers, and you want to create a new list containing the squares of those numbers. Here's how you can do it with list comprehension:

```
numbers = [1, 2, 3, 4, 5]
squares = [x**2 for x in numbers]
```

### Example 2: Filtering Even Numbers

Let's say you have a list of numbers, and you want to create a new list containing only the even numbers:

```
numbers = [1, 2, 3, 4, 5, 6, 7, 8, 9, 10]
even_numbers = [x for x in numbers if x % 2 == 0]
```

### Example 3: Combining Two Lists

You can also use list comprehension to combine elements from two lists:

```
fruits = ["apple", "banana", "cherry"]
colors = ["red", "yellow", "red"]
fruit_colors = [f"{fruit} is {color}" for fruit, color in zip(fruits, colors)]
```

## Nesting and Advanced List Comprehension

List comprehensions can be nested, allowing you to work with multi-dimensional data structures like matrices. You can also use more complex expressions and conditions to handle more intricate data transformations.

## When to Use List Comprehension

List comprehension is an excellent choice when you want to create a new list based on an existing iterable. However, for complex operations or when you need to modify the original iterable, traditional for loops may be more suitable.

## Conclusion

List comprehension is a powerful Python feature that simplifies and streamlines the process of creating lists. It's a tool you'll find yourself reaching for frequently in your Python programming journey, whether you're working with data, filtering elements, or performing transformations. As you continue to explore Python web scraping, remember the elegance and efficiency that list comprehension can bring to your code.

# Chapter 3: Web Scraping Fundamentals

Welcome to Chapter 3, where we'll dive headfirst into the exciting world of web scraping! In the previous chapters, we've laid a strong foundation in Python programming, including the use of variables, conditional statements, loops, and even the elegance of list comprehensions. Now, it's time to take your Python skills to the next level and explore the art and science of web scraping.

## Uncovering the Secrets of the Web

The internet is a vast treasure trove of information, with countless websites offering valuable data, insights, and resources. Web scraping is the art of systematically extracting this information from websites and transforming it into structured, usable data. Whether you're a researcher seeking academic articles, a business analyst tracking market trends, or a curious tinkerer exploring the web's vast landscape, web scraping opens doors to a wealth of possibilities.

## Building Blocks of Web Scraping

In this chapter, we'll begin by laying the foundational building blocks of web scraping. We'll start with an exploration of the Hypertext Transfer Protocol (HTTP), the language of the web. Understanding how web communication works through HTTP requests and responses is essential for effective web scraping.

Next, we'll delve into the anatomy of a Uniform Resource Locator (URL), the web addresses that guide us to specific online resources. Unraveling the components of a URL will enable you to navigate the web with precision and target the data you seek.

## Meet BeautifulSoup and `requests`

As we embark on our web scraping journey, we'll introduce you to two powerful tools that will be your faithful companions throughout this chapter and beyond:

- **BeautifulSoup:** This Python library specializes in parsing HTML and XML documents, allowing you to navigate and extract data effortlessly. You'll become adept at using BeautifulSoup to dissect web pages and extract the information you desire.
- **`requests` Library:** A versatile Python library that facilitates making HTTP requests, `requests` will be your gateway to the web. You'll discover how to fetch web pages, interact with servers, and retrieve valuable data programmatically.

## Hands-on Examples and Practical Skills

To ensure your understanding, we'll guide you through hands-on examples of web scraping. We'll start with simple exercises, gradually progressing to more complex tasks. You'll learn how to scrape quotes, gather news headlines, and extract product prices, all while applying the principles and techniques introduced in this chapter.

# Building Blocks of Web Scraping

Now that we've set the stage for our journey into web scraping, it's time to lay down the essential building blocks that will empower you to navigate the web's vast terrain effectively. Think of these building blocks as the keys to unlocking the treasure chest of online data.

## Understanding HTTP: The Language of the Web

Before we can scrape data from websites, we must first understand the language of the web—HTTP, the Hypertext Transfer Protocol. Imagine it as the messenger that facilitates conversations between your web browser and the servers hosting the websites you visit. In this section, we'll delve into the core concepts of HTTP:

- **Request-Response Paradigm:** We'll explore how web communication revolves around a simple request-response cycle. Every time you load a webpage, you're essentially sending a request to a server, and the server responds with the requested data.
- **Status Codes and Headers:** HTTP responses carry valuable information in the form of status codes and headers. These codes tell us whether the request was successful or encountered an error, while headers provide details about the data being sent, such as content type and encoding.
- **HTTP Methods:** HTTP defines various methods (or verbs) that dictate the action to be performed on a resource. You'll become familiar with the most common methods, like GET for retrieval and POST for data submission.
- **Statelessness:** HTTP is inherently stateless, which means each request-response interaction is independent. While this simplicity is advantageous, it requires mechanisms like cookies and sessions to maintain user state.

## Demystifying the URL

Next on our journey, we'll unravel the mysteries of the Uniform Resource Locator (URL), which serves as our guide through the intricate web of online resources. Think of URLs as the GPS coordinates of the internet, pointing us to specific locations. Here's what we'll discover:

- **Scheme:** This is the protocol used for communication, whether it's the familiar "http" or the secure "https."
- **Domain:** The domain, often starting with "www," reveals the host or server where the resource resides. It's like the street address for a webpage.
- **Port:** While often omitted, the port number specifies the communication channel on the server. "80" for HTTP and "443" for HTTPS are common examples.
- **Path:** The path is the route to the resource on the server's file system or within an application. It's akin to navigating a directory structure.
- **Query:** Queries are like instructions for customization, allowing us to tailor our requests with parameters like search terms or filters.
- **Fragment:** Fragments help us pinpoint specific sections within a resource, akin to bookmarks within a book.

As we master these building blocks, you'll gain a solid understanding of web communication and be well-prepared to embark on our practical journey into web scraping.

In the next sections, we'll introduce you to two trusty companions that will aid you in this endeavor: BeautifulSoup and the `requests` library. These tools will become your allies in parsing web content and fetching data from the vast digital landscape. So, stay tuned as we explore the practical side of web scraping and unravel the secrets hidden within the web's pages.

## Request-Response Paradigm: Navigating the Web's Conversations

In the vast realm of the internet, web communication follows a fundamental pattern known as the "Request-Response Paradigm." Imagine it as a conversation between you, the web browser user, and the servers hosting the websites you visit. Understanding this paradigm is like deciphering the language of the web itself.

## The Art of Requesting

### Every Web Page Load is a Request

Picture this: Every time you click a link, enter a web address, or submit a search query, you're effectively sending a request to a web server. It's akin to politely asking, "Could you please provide me with this specific piece of information?" This request, in the realm of the web, is typically initiated by your web browser.

### Types of Requests

There are various types of requests, each serving a distinct purpose. The most common one you'll encounter is the "GET" request. It's used to retrieve data—think of it as a way to ask for information or resources. Other request types, like "POST," "PUT," "PATCH," and "DELETE," are used for actions such as submitting forms, updating data, or deleting content.

## The Magic of Responses

### When the Server Responds

Once your request reaches the web server, the server processes it and then sends back a response. This response contains the requested data or information, and it's essentially the server's reply to your inquiry. Think of it as the server saying, "Here's what you asked for."

## Status Codes and Headers: Deciphering the Server's Language

### Status Codes: The Server's Mood Indicator

Now, here's where it gets interesting. In this response, there's a small but essential piece of information known as the "status code." It's like the server's way of letting you know how things went. Status codes come in three digits and convey crucial information about the request's outcome:

- **2xx:** These codes indicate success. For example, "200 OK" tells you that your request was successful, and you're getting the data you wanted.
- **3xx:** These codes signify redirection. They might tell you that the resource has moved temporarily (e.g., "302 Found") or permanently (e.g., "301 Moved Permanently").
- **4xx:** When you see a 4xx status code, it means there was an issue with your request. "404 Not Found" is perhaps the most famous of these, indicating that the requested resource couldn't be located.
- **5xx:** These codes hint at server errors. If you encounter a "500 Internal Server Error," it means something went wrong on the server's side.

### Headers: The Extra Information

In addition to status codes, HTTP responses also include something called "headers." Think of headers as additional notes or annotations attached to the server's response. They provide valuable details about the data being sent, such as the content type (e.g., HTML or JSON), the character encoding, and more. Headers help your web browser understand how to process and display the received data correctly.

## Navigating the Web's Conversations

So, every time you click a link or type a web address, you're initiating a request that travels to a web server. The server processes your request, responds with data, and provides a status code to indicate the outcome. Headers accompany this response, offering extra information about the data.

Understanding this request-response paradigm and deciphering status codes and headers is fundamental to effective web scraping. It's akin to learning the language of the web, allowing you to navigate and interact with online resources intelligently. Armed with this knowledge, you're now ready to dive deeper into the world of web scraping, unlocking the secrets hidden within the web's pages.

## Demystifying the URL: Navigating the Digital Terrain

Now, let's embark on a journey to demystify one of the most fundamental elements of the web: the Uniform Resource Locator (URL). Think of URLs as your trusty GPS coordinates in the vast landscape of the internet. They guide you to specific online locations, much like street addresses lead you to physical destinations. As we unravel the intricacies of URLs, you'll gain a deeper understanding of how the web operates.

### Scheme: The Protocol of Communication

At the heart of every URL lies the **scheme**, which defines the protocol used for communication. You've likely encountered the familiar "http" or its secure counterpart, "https." The scheme sets the rules for how your web browser interacts with the server. For example, "http" instructs your browser to use the standard HTTP protocol, while "https" signals a secure, encrypted connection. Let's take a closer look at a couple of examples using Craigslist:

- **HTTP Scheme:** http://www.craigslist.com
- **HTTPS Scheme:** https://secure.craigslist.com

These schemes dictate how data is transmitted and ensure secure communication when needed.

## Domain: The Web's Hosts and Servers

Moving on, the **domain** is the star of the show in a URL. It's the part that often starts with "www" and reveals the host or server where the desired resource resides. Think of it as the street address for a webpage. Here are a couple of examples using Craigslist:

- **Standard Domain:** https://www.logrocket.com/
- **Subdomain:** https://accounts.craigslist.org/login

Domains help route your request to the correct destination on the internet. They can be as simple as "craigslist.com" or as specific as " https://accounts.craigslist.org/login" indicating different sections or services hosted on the same server.

## Port: The Communication Channel

While often tucked away behind the scenes, the **port** number plays a crucial role in web communication. It specifies the channel on the server through which your request should be processed. By default, "80" is the port for HTTP, while "443" is the secure port for HTTPS. Here's a glimpse using Craigslist:

- **HTTP Port:** http://www.craigslist.com:80
- **HTTPS Port:** https://secure.craigslist.com:443

Although port numbers are often omitted in URLs, they ensure that your request arrives at the right door on the server.

## Path: Navigating the Digital Landscape

Now, let's delve into the **path**, which is like the route to a treasure hidden on the server's file system or within an application. It's akin to navigating a directory structure on your computer. Paths guide your request to the specific resource you seek. For instance, when searching for classifieds on Craigslist:

- **Resource Path:** https://newyork.craigslist.org/search/zip#search=1~gallery~0~0
- **File Path:** https://images.craigslist.org/00M0M_7V2Fw4hfhh0_0t20CI_300x300.jpg

Paths help you pinpoint the precise location of the desired data or resource.

## Query: Tailoring Requests

URLs can also carry **queries**, which are like instructions for customization. Queries are expressed as key-value pairs, allowing you to tailor your requests with parameters such as search terms, filters, or configuration options. Here's how queries look when searching for apartments on Craigslist:

- **Search Query:** https://newyork.craigslist.org/search/apa
- **Filter Query:** https://newyork.craigslist.org/search/apa?max_price=2000

Queries empower you to interact with web applications dynamically, customizing your experience as you navigate the web.

## Fragment: Pinpointing Sections

Lastly, let's uncover **fragments**, which serve as your bookmarks within a digital resource. Fragments allow you to pinpoint specific sections within a resource, much like flipping to a specific page in a book. They are often used in web pages to scroll to specific sections or highlight particular content. Here's an example when exploring articles on Craigslist:

- **Fragment Identifier:** https://newyork.craigslist.org/search/pet

Fragments offer a precise way to navigate lengthy documents and find the information you need quickly.

## Experimenting with Curl

To experiment with web endpoints and gain a deeper understanding of how URLs work, you can use a tool like `curl` (short for "Client URL") from your command line. `Curl` allows you to send HTTP requests directly to web servers, providing you with insights into the web's inner workings. For instance, you can use `curl` to send a GET request to a webpage and observe the HTTP response, including status codes and headers.

Here's an example of using `curl` to fetch the content of a Craigslist webpage:

```
curl -L http://www.craigslist.com
```

By experimenting with `curl` and different Craigslist URLs, you can explore various web endpoints, observe the responses they generate, and deepen your understanding of web communication.

As we navigate the web's terrain and demystify its components, you'll find that URLs are your compass in this digital world.

## Meet BeautifulSoup and `requests`: Your Navigators in Web Scraping

Now that we've unraveled the essentials of URLs and web communication, it's time to introduce you to two trusty companions that will be your guides and allies in the art of web scraping. Meet BeautifulSoup and the `requests` library, your navigators through the intricate structures of web pages and your gateways to the vast digital landscape of information.

## BeautifulSoup: Unveiling the Beauty of HTML and XML

Imagine you're handed a book written in a foreign language, and you need to extract specific information from it. This is precisely the scenario web scraping often presents, where web pages are coded in the language of HTML (Hypertext Markup Language) or XML (eXtensible Markup Language). BeautifulSoup is your linguistic expert, your interpreter in this digital world.

## What is a `<div>`?

Before we dive deeper into BeautifulSoup, let's understand an essential concept: the HTML `<div>` element. In the language of web development, a `<div>` is like a container, a box that holds content or groups elements together. It stands for "division" and is a fundamental building block of web page layout and structure. For example, a website might use a `<div>` to define the header, another for the main content area, and yet another for the footer.

```html
<div id="header">
    <h1>Welcome to My Website</h1>
    <p>Explore the World of Web Scraping</p>
</div>

<div id="content">
    <h2>Latest Articles</h2>
    <ul>
        <li>Article 1: Introduction to Web Scraping</li>
        <li>Article 2: Mastering BeautifulSoup</li>
        <li>Article 3: Advanced Scraping Techniques</li>
    </ul>
</div>

<div id="footer">
    <p>&copy; 2023 MyWebsite.com</p>
</div>
```

In the example above, we have three `<div>` elements - one for the header, one for the content, and one for the footer. Each `<div>` serves as a container for specific sections of the web page, making it easier to style and manipulate these sections.

## BeautifulSoup: Your HTML Interpreter

Now, let's return to BeautifulSoup. This Python library is your HTML interpreter, capable of dissecting web pages like a skilled surgeon. It can navigate the intricate structures of HTML and XML documents, helping you locate and extract the information you desire. For instance, if you want to scrape the article titles from the example web page above, BeautifulSoup allows you to target the `<ul>` element within the `<div id="content">`, then extract each `<li>` item within it.

```python
# Sample BeautifulSoup code for extracting article titles
from bs4 import BeautifulSoup

# Sample HTML content (replace with actual web page content)
html_content = """
<div id="content">
    <h2>Latest Articles</h2>
    <ul>
        <li>Article 1: Introduction to Web Scraping</li>
        <li>Article 2: Mastering BeautifulSoup</li>
        <li>Article 3: Advanced Scraping Techniques</li>
    </ul>
</div>
"""

# Create a BeautifulSoup object
soup = BeautifulSoup(html_content, 'html.parser')

# Find the <div> with id="content"
content_div = soup.find('div', {'id': 'content'})

# Find all <li> items within the <ul> element
article_titles = [li.text for li in content_div.find('ul').find_all('li')]

print(article_titles)
```

With BeautifulSoup, you can traverse the HTML structure, locate specific elements, extract their content, and organize it for further analysis or storage.

### `requests` Library: Your Gateway to the Web

Now, let's meet your gateway to the web, the `requests` library. It's like your personal courier, capable of sending and receiving messages from web servers. With the `requests` library, you can make HTTP requests to fetch web pages, interact with remote servers, and retrieve valuable data programmatically.

Here's a simple example of using the `requests` library to fetch the content of a real website, such as "http://www.craigslist.com":

```python
import requests

# Send a GET request to a website
response = requests.get("http://www.craigslist.com")

# Print the response content
print(response.text)
```

The `requests` library makes it easy to fetch web pages and access their content. In this example, we've sent a GET request to Craigslist's website, and the response object contains the HTML content of the page. This is just the beginning; you can use `requests` to interact with web servers, send data, and retrieve information from websites.

As we progress through this chapter, you'll become well-acquainted with BeautifulSoup and the `requests` library. Together, they'll be your indispensable tools for exploring the web's vast resources, extracting valuable data, and embarking on exciting web scraping adventures. So, get ready to unleash the power of Python and these tools as we dive deeper into the world of web scraping!

## Extracting Data from HTML Tables Using BeautifulSoup

HTML tables are a common way to organize and display structured data on web pages. When it comes to web scraping, extracting data from these tables is a valuable skill. In this section, we'll explore how to use BeautifulSoup to navigate and extract data from an HTML table.

## Understanding HTML Tables

Before we dive into the code, let's take a moment to understand the basic structure of an HTML table. HTML tables consist of rows (`<tr>`) and columns (`<td>` or `<th>`). Here's a simple example:

```
<table>
    <tr>
        <th>Name</th>
        <th>Age</th>
        <th>City</th>
    </tr>
    <tr>
        <td>John</td>
        <td>30</td>
        <td>New York</td>
    </tr>
    <tr>
        <td>Alice</td>
        <td>25</td>
        <td>San Francisco</td>
    </tr>
</table>
```

In this example, we have a table with three columns: "Name," "Age," and "City." The first row contains table headers (`<th>`), and the subsequent rows contain data cells (`<td>`).

## Extracting Data with BeautifulSoup

To extract data from an HTML table using BeautifulSoup, follow these steps:

1. Parse the HTML content using BeautifulSoup.
2. Locate the table element by using the `find()` method.
3. Navigate through the rows and columns of the table to extract data.

Here's a Python code example that demonstrates how to extract data from the HTML table above:

```python
from bs4 import BeautifulSoup

# Sample HTML content with the table
html_content = """
<table>
    <tr>
        <th>Name</th>
        <th>Age</th>
        <th>City</th>
    </tr>
    <tr>
        <td>John</td>
        <td>30</td>
        <td>New York</td>
    </tr>
    <tr>
        <td>Alice</td>
        <td>25</td>
        <td>San Francisco</td>
    </tr>
</table>
"""

# Create a BeautifulSoup object
soup = BeautifulSoup(html_content, 'html.parser')

# Find the table element
table = soup.find('table')

# Initialize empty lists to store data
data = []
headers = []

# Extract table headers
for th in table.find('tr').find_all('th'):
    headers.append(th.text)

# Extract table rows and data
for row in table.find_all('tr')[1:]:  # Start from the second row to skip headers
    row_data = []
    for cell in row.find_all('td'):
        row_data.append(cell.text)
```

```
        data.append(row_data)

# Print headers and data
print("Headers:", headers)
print("Data:", data)
```

In this example, we first locate the table element using `soup.find('table')`. Then, we iterate through the rows and columns, extracting the data into lists. The `headers` list contains the table headers, and the `data` list contains the data from the table rows.

By following this approach, you can extract data from HTML tables on web pages and use it for various purposes, such as analysis, reporting, or further processing. BeautifulSoup simplifies the process of navigating and extracting data from HTML, making web scraping tasks more manageable.

# Parsing Different Types of Markup: Unveiling the Parsing Power of BeautifulSoup

In the world of web scraping, understanding the various types of markup and how to parse them is crucial. BeautifulSoup, our trusty companion, excels at handling different markup languages, such as HTML and XML, with grace and precision. In this section, we'll explore the parsing capabilities of BeautifulSoup, shedding light on its versatile parsers and their ideal use cases.

## Embracing Markup Diversity

The web is a vast and diverse ecosystem, and web pages can be constructed using different markup languages. The two most common types you'll encounter are:

### 1. HTML (Hypertext Markup Language)

HTML is the foundation of web pages, defining the structure and content of a document. It's the language that gives structure to the web, specifying how elements like headings, paragraphs, links, and images are displayed and interacted with.

### 2. XML (eXtensible Markup Language)

XML is a flexible markup language often used to structure and transport data. It doesn't define how data should be displayed like HTML; instead, it focuses on describing data's structure and meaning. XML is prevalent in various contexts, including data exchange formats and configuration files.

## The Power of Parsers

BeautifulSoup empowers you to parse both HTML and XML seamlessly. However, it provides multiple parsers to choose from, each with its advantages and use cases. Let's explore the parsers available:

### 1. 'html.parser'

- **Benefits:** This parser is included with Python's standard library, making it convenient to use without installing additional dependencies. It's a good choice for parsing well-formed HTML.
- **Use Cases:** Use 'html.parser' when dealing with HTML documents that adhere to the standard and have consistent formatting.

### 2. 'lxml'

- **Benefits:** 'lxml' is a third-party library known for its speed and flexibility. It can handle both HTML and XML, making it a versatile choice. It's particularly useful for parsing complex or large documents.
- **Use Cases:** Opt for 'lxml' when dealing with HTML or XML documents that may have irregular formatting, complex structures, or when parsing speed is crucial.

## 3. 'xml'

- **Benefits:** The 'xml' parser is designed specifically for parsing XML documents. It's lightweight and efficient for processing structured data.
- **Use Cases:** Choose 'xml' when parsing XML documents that require minimal overhead and when you need to focus solely on the data's structure.

# Example: Parsing HTML with 'lxml'

Let's demonstrate how to use the 'lxml' parser to parse HTML:

```
from bs4 import BeautifulSoup

# Sample HTML content
html_content = """
<html>
<head>
    <title>Sample HTML Page</title>
</head>
<body>
    <h1>Welcome to BeautifulSoup</h1>
    <p>This is a sample HTML document.</p>
</body>
</html>
"""

# Create a BeautifulSoup object using 'lxml' parser
soup = BeautifulSoup(html_content, 'lxml')

# Extract and print the title element
title_element = soup.title
print("Title:", title_element.text)

# Extract and print the paragraph element
paragraph_element = soup.p
print("Paragraph:", paragraph_element.text)
```

In this example, we use the 'lxml' parser to parse an HTML document. We then extract and print the title and paragraph elements from the parsed content.

By understanding the diverse types of markup and selecting the appropriate parser, you'll be well-prepared to tackle web scraping tasks across a wide range of web pages and data formats.

BeautifulSoup's parsing capabilities, combined with the right parser, empower you to extract valuable data with precision and efficiency.

# Chapter 4: Navigating and Parsing with BeautifulSoup

Welcome to an exciting chapter where we dive deeper into the world of BeautifulSoup, equipping you with essential skills to navigate the HTML tree, parse different types of markup, and harness the power of CSS selectors. As we journey through these topics, you'll gain the expertise to wield BeautifulSoup like a true web scraping maestro.

## Navigating the HTML Tree

Understanding how to navigate the HTML tree is crucial for extracting specific data from web pages effectively. BeautifulSoup provides a variety of methods to traverse the DOM (Document Object Model) and access elements precisely where they reside. We'll explore some of these methods:

## The find() Method

With the `find()` method, you can locate the first occurrence of an element that matches your criteria. Whether you're looking for a specific tag, attribute, or text content, `find()` is your trusty guide. Here's a taste of how it works:

```
# Find the first <a> tag with a specific class
link = soup.find('a', class_='my-link')
```

## The find_all() Method

Sometimes, one isn't enough. When you need to gather multiple elements that fit your criteria, turn to `find_all()`. It returns a list of all matching elements, opening the door to data extraction at scale:

```
# Find all <li> elements within an <ul> list
list_items = soup.find_all('li')
```

## Parent and siblings

Let's delve into the concept of "next siblings" in BeautifulSoup and see how we can use it to extract elements from a mock HTML file.

Consider the following mock HTML file:

```
<!DOCTYPE html>
<html>
<head>
    <title>Mock HTML Page</title>
</head>
```

```
<body>
    <div id="content">
        <h1>Welcome to Our Website</h1>
        <p>This is a sample web page.</p>
        <ul>
            <li>Item 1</li>
            <li>Item 2</li>
            <li>Item 3</li>
        </ul>
        <p>More content here.</p>
    </div>
</body>
</html>
```

In this example, we have a simple HTML structure with a `<div>` element containing various child elements.

Let's use BeautifulSoup to navigate and extract elements, focusing on the concept of "next siblings."

```python
from bs4 import BeautifulSoup

# Mock HTML content
html_content = """
<!DOCTYPE html>
<html>
<head>
    <title>Mock HTML Page</title>
</head>
<body>
    <div id="content">
        <h1>Welcome to Our Website</h1>
        <p>This is a sample web page.</p>
        <ul>
            <li>Item 1</li>
            <li>Item 2</li>
            <li>Item 3</li>
        </ul>
        <p>More content here.</p>
    </div>
</body>
</html>
"""

# Create a BeautifulSoup object
soup = BeautifulSoup(html_content, 'html.parser')

# Find the <ul> element
ul_element = soup.find('ul')

# Extract the <li> items using next_sibling
li_items = ul_element.next_sibling.find_all('li')

# Print the text of <li> items
for item in li_items:
```

```
print(item.text)
```

In this code:

1. We create a BeautifulSoup object, `soup`, to parse the mock HTML content.
2. We find the `<ul>` element using `soup.find('ul')`.
3. Next, we use the `next_sibling` attribute to access the next sibling of the `<ul>` element, which is the `<p>` element containing "More content here."
4. Finally, we use `find_all('li')` to extract all the `<li>` items within the `<p>` element, and we print their text content.

When you run this code, it will output:

```
Item 1
Item 2
Item 3
```

This demonstrates how you can use the "next siblings" concept in BeautifulSoup to navigate the HTML tree and extract specific elements following a target element. It allows you to access and manipulate elements sequentially within the same parent element.

# Working with CSS Selectors: Unleashing the Power of Precision

In the world of web scraping, precision is key. BeautifulSoup equips you with a powerful tool: CSS selectors. In this section, we'll dive into the realm of CSS selectors and demonstrate how they can be harnessed using BeautifulSoup's `select()` method to precisely target and extract elements from web pages.

## The Magic of CSS Selectors

Cascading Style Sheets (CSS) selectors are like a finely tuned instrument in the world of web design and development. They are used to apply styles to specific elements on a web page. However, we can use the same selectors to navigate and extract elements with surgical precision.

## Selecting by Class

Let's start with one of the most common scenarios: selecting elements by their class attribute. In HTML, elements can have one or more classes assigned to them. CSS selectors allow us to target elements with a specific class.

Consider this mock HTML snippet:

```
<div class="container">
    <p class="highlight">This is a highlighted paragraph.</p>
    <p>This is a regular paragraph.</p>
</div>
```

To select the `<p>` element with the class "highlight," we can use the CSS selector `.highlight`:

```python
from bs4 import BeautifulSoup

# Sample HTML content
html_content = """
<div class="container">
    <p class="highlight">This is a highlighted paragraph.</p>
    <p>This is a regular paragraph.</p>
</div>
"""

# Create a BeautifulSoup object
soup = BeautifulSoup(html_content, 'html.parser')

# Select elements with class "highlight"
highlighted_paragraph = soup.select('.highlight')

# Print the text of the selected element
print("Highlighted Paragraph:", highlighted_paragraph[0].text)
```

## Selecting by ID

Another powerful selector is targeting elements by their unique ID attribute. IDs should be unique within a document, making them excellent for precise selections.

Consider this HTML snippet:

```html
<div id="header">
    <h1>Welcome to Our Website</h1>
</div>
```

To select the `<h1>` element with the ID "header," we can use the CSS selector `#header`:

```python
from bs4 import BeautifulSoup

# Sample HTML content
html_content = """
<div id="header">
    <h1>Welcome to Our Website</h1>
</div>
"""

# Create a BeautifulSoup object
soup = BeautifulSoup(html_content, 'html.parser')

# Select elements with ID "header"
header_element = soup.select('#header')

# Print the text of the selected element
print("Header Text:", header_element[0].text)
```

## Selecting by Element Type

Finally, we can select elements by their HTML element type. This selector is handy when you want to target all elements of a particular type on a page.

Consider this HTML snippet:

```html
<ul>
    <li>Item 1</li>
    <li>Item 2</li>
    <li>Item 3</li>
</ul>
```

To select all `<li>` elements within the `<ul>`, we can use the CSS selector `ul li`:

```python
from bs4 import BeautifulSoup

# Sample HTML content
html_content = """
```

```
<ul>
    <li>Item 1</li>
    <li>Item 2</li>
    <li>Item 3</li>
</ul>
"""

# Create a BeautifulSoup object
soup = BeautifulSoup(html_content, 'html.parser')

# Select all <li> elements within <ul>
list_items = soup.select('ul li')

# Print the text of the selected elements
for item in list_items:
    print("List Item:", item.text)
```

These examples demonstrate how CSS selectors, when combined with BeautifulSoup's `select()` method, empower you to precisely target and extract elements from web pages. Whether it's selecting by class, ID, or element type, CSS selectors provide the finesse needed to navigate web pages with confidence and accuracy.

# Chapter 5: Unleashing the Power of Web Scraping

In the previous chapters, we laid the groundwork for your Python journey, mastering variables, conditional statements, loops, and even delving into the elegance of list comprehensions. Now, we're about to embark on a thrilling adventure into the world of web scraping—a skill that can open doors to a treasure trove of data and insights.

## Introduction to Chapter 5

In this chapter, we're going to explore the practical applications of web scraping, and trust me, they are limitless. Web scraping isn't just a neat trick; it's a game-changer in various fields, from market research to data analysis, and everything in between.

## Market Research: Unveiling Hidden Insights

We'll kick things off by diving into the fascinating world of market research. Imagine having the ability to collect real-time data from e-commerce websites, social media platforms, or customer review websites. With web scraping, you can do just that. We'll explore how web scraping can:

- **Monitor Competitors:** Keep a close eye on your competitors' prices, product offerings, and customer reviews. This information is invaluable in making informed business decisions.
- **Gauge Customer Sentiment:** Scrub the web for user-generated reviews and comments to gauge customer sentiment about your products or services. Are customers happy? What improvements do they suggest?
- **Identify Trends:** Spot emerging trends by analyzing data from various sources, giving you a competitive edge in adapting to changing market conditions.
- **Collect Pricing Data:** Automatically collect pricing information for products across different e-commerce websites. This data can be used for price optimization strategies.

But that's just the beginning! In the following sections of this chapter, we'll delve into more diverse and intriguing applications of web scraping. From academic research and data journalism to content aggregation and business intelligence, web scraping will become your go-to tool for accessing and analyzing valuable information on the internet.

So, fasten your seatbelt and get ready to uncover the potential of web scraping. Whether you're a researcher, a journalist, a business owner, or a curious tinkerer, the world of web scraping has something in store for you. Let's dive in!

## Real World Example

Lets do a real world example to get all the product titles and prices from a dog cake baking website

```
import re
```

```python
import requests
from bs4 import BeautifulSoup

# Make a request to the website
url = "https://www.itssofluffybakery.com/collections/dogs"
response = requests.get(url)

# Parse the HTML content
soup = BeautifulSoup(response.content, "html.parser")

# Find all product containers
products = soup.find_all("a", class_="product-grid-item")

# Extract product information for each product
for product in products:
    # Get the product title
    title = product.find("p").text.strip()

    # Extract the price
    price_tag = product.find("div", class_="product-item--price").find("small")
    # price_text = price_tag.text.strip()
    price_text = price_tag.text.strip()
    price = price_text[:-2]
    cents = price_text[-2:]

    print(f"Title: {title}")
    print(f"Price: {price}.{cents}")
    print("---")
```

```
> python3 market_research.py
Title: Small Circle MEAT LOVER
Price: $23.99
---
Title: Medium Bone
Price: $28.99
---
Title: Small Bone
Price: $20.99
---
Title: Medium Bone MEAT LOVER
Price: $31.99
---
Title: Paw
Price: $33.99
---
Title: Small Bone MEAT LOVER
Price: $23.99
---
Title: Unicorn Cake
Price: $35.99
---
Title: Big Bone
Price: $32.99
---
```

Title: Party Hats (Boy/Girl)
Price: $5.99
---
Title: Small Butterfly Cake
Price: $26.99
---
Title: Paw MEAT LOVER
Price: $37.99
---
Title: Christmas Lunchbox (sm)
Price: $9.99

# Dealing with Dynamic Web Pages: Taming the JavaScript Beast

In the world of web scraping, not all web pages are created equal. Some are straightforward, static, and willingly give up their data upon request. However, there's another breed of web pages—the dynamic ones. These pages play hard to get, relying on JavaScript to load and manipulate content after the initial page load. In this section, we'll confront the challenges posed by dynamic web pages and unveil the tools and strategies to conquer them.

## The Dynamic Web Page Dilemma

Dynamic web pages are a double-edged sword. They provide an interactive and seamless user experience by fetching and rendering data on-the-fly using JavaScript. While this is fantastic for users, it complicates web scraping efforts. When you make a traditional HTTP request to a dynamic page, you often receive only the initial HTML shell, devoid of the dynamic content you seek.

Consider a mock web page that loads data dynamically using JavaScript:

```html
<!DOCTYPE html>
<html>
<head>
    <title>Dynamic Web Page</title>
</head>
<body>
    <div id="content">
        <h1>Welcome to the Dynamic Page</h1>
        <button onclick="loadData()">Load Data</button>
        <div id="dynamicData"></div>
    </div>

    <script>
        function loadData() {
            // Simulate data loading with a delay
            setTimeout(function() {
                const dynamicDataDiv =
document.getElementById("dynamicData");
                dynamicDataDiv.innerHTML = "<p>This is dynamically loaded
data.</p>";
            }, 2000); // Simulate a 2-second delay
        }
    </script>
</body>
</html>
```

In this example, clicking the "Load Data" button triggers a JavaScript function that loads data into the dynamicData div after a 2-second delay. If you attempt to scrape this page with traditional methods, you'll miss out on the dynamically loaded content.

## Enter Selenium: The JavaScript Whisperer

To overcome the challenges of dynamic web pages, we introduce Selenium, a powerful tool in the web scraping arsenal. Selenium is a browser automation framework that allows you to script interactions with web pages, just as a human user would. It's particularly handy for dealing with pages that rely heavily on JavaScript.

With Selenium, you can:

- **Simulate User Actions:** Interact with web elements, click buttons, fill out forms, and scroll.
- **Wait for Dynamic Content:** Pause execution until the dynamic content has loaded.
- **Retrieve Dynamic Data:** Scrape data from pages that rely on JavaScript to render content.

Here's a snippet of Python code that uses Selenium to scrape data from our mock dynamic web page:

```python
from selenium import webdriver
from selenium.webdriver.common.by import By
from selenium.webdriver.common.keys import Keys
import time

# Initialize a Selenium webdriver (you'll need to download the appropriate driver)
driver = webdriver.Chrome(executable_path='/path/to/chromedriver')

# Open the dynamic web page
driver.get("https://localhost:3000/dynamic-page")

# Click the "Load Data" button
load_button = driver.find_element(By.XPATH, "//button[contains(text(), 'Load Data')]")
load_button.click()

# Wait for the dynamic data to load (you may need to adjust the wait time)
time.sleep(2)

# Extract the dynamically loaded data
dynamic_data = driver.find_element(By.ID, "dynamicData").text

# Print the dynamic data
print("Dynamic Data:", dynamic_data)

# Close the browser
driver.quit()
```

In this example, we use Selenium to open the dynamic web page, click the "Load Data" button, wait for the data to load, and then extract and print the dynamically loaded content.

## When to Use Selenium with BeautifulSoup

While Selenium is an excellent tool for dealing with dynamic web pages, it comes with additional complexity and overhead. Therefore, it's essential to consider when to use Selenium in conjunction with BeautifulSoup:

1. **Use BeautifulSoup First:** If the page contains static content or data that's readily available in the initial HTML response, start with BeautifulSoup. It's faster and more efficient for parsing static content.
2. **Reserve Selenium for Dynamic Elements:** Use Selenium when dealing with pages that rely heavily on JavaScript for data retrieval and rendering. It's your go-to solution when traditional scraping methods fall short.

By combining the powers of BeautifulSoup and Selenium, you can tackle the most challenging web scraping scenarios, from simple static pages to complex dynamic ones. So, whether you're dealing with the straightforward or the elusive, you have the tools and knowledge needed to conquer the dynamic web.

## Installing ChromeDriver on Mac and Linux

ChromeDriver is a crucial component when using Selenium for web scraping or browser automation tasks. It allows Selenium to communicate with the Google Chrome browser. In this section, we'll guide you through the installation process of ChromeDriver on both Mac and Linux operating systems.

## Installation on Mac

## Step 1: Check Your Chrome Browser Version

Before installing ChromeDriver, ensure that you have Google Chrome installed on your Mac. You'll need to match the version of ChromeDriver with your Chrome browser version.

1. Open Google Chrome.
2. Click on the three vertical dots (menu) in the top-right corner.
3. Go to "Help" > "About Google Chrome."

Note down the version number, which will be displayed on the "About Chrome" page.

## Step 2: Download ChromeDriver

Now that you know your Chrome browser version, visit the official ChromeDriver download page: https://sites.google.com/chromium.org/driver/

1. Find the version of ChromeDriver that matches your Chrome browser version.

2. Click on the download link next to your version to download the ChromeDriver binary.

### Step 3: Install ChromeDriver

1. Once the download is complete, unzip the downloaded file.
2. You'll have the `chromedriver` binary file. To make it available system-wide, move it to a directory listed in your system's PATH. A common location is `/usr/local/bin`:

```
sudo mv chromedriver /usr/local/bin/
```

3. Make `chromedriver` executable:

```
sudo chmod +x /usr/local/bin/chromedriver
```

4. Verify the installation by running the following command:

```
chromedriver --version
```

This should display the ChromeDriver version you installed.

## Installation on Linux (Ubuntu/Debian)

### Step 1: Check Your Chrome Browser Version

Just like on Mac, ensure that you have Google Chrome installed on your Linux system and note down the version.

### Step 2: Download ChromeDriver

Visit the official ChromeDriver download page: https://sites.google.com/chromium.org/driver/

1. Find the version of ChromeDriver that matches your Chrome browser version.
2. Click on the download link next to your version to download the ChromeDriver binary.

### Step 3: Install ChromeDriver

1. Unzip the downloaded file to extract the `chromedriver` binary.
2. Move `chromedriver` to a directory listed in your system's PATH. A common location is `/usr/local/bin`:

```
sudo mv chromedriver /usr/local/bin/
```

3. Make `chromedriver` executable:

```
sudo chmod +x /usr/local/bin/chromedriver
```

4. Verify the installation by running the following command:

```
chromedriver --version
```

This should display the ChromeDriver version you installed.

## Conclusion

With ChromeDriver successfully installed on your Mac or Linux system, you're now ready to use Selenium for web scraping and browser automation tasks with Google Chrome. Make sure to match the ChromeDriver version with your Chrome browser version to ensure compatibility. Happy web scraping!

# Chapter 6: Introduction to Chrome Inspector

## Overview of Chrome Inspector

Welcome to the fascinating world of web scraping, where the Chrome Inspector plays a pivotal role. Imagine the Chrome Inspector as your digital magnifying glass, allowing you to peer into the intricate details of web pages. It's a tool embedded in Google Chrome, widely used by developers and web scraping enthusiasts to examine and modify the HTML and CSS of a page, monitor network activity, and much more.

The Chrome Inspector is not just a tool; it's a gateway to understanding how web pages are structured and how they function. When you scrape a website, knowing where and how the data is presented is crucial. The Inspector provides you with this insight, making it an indispensable tool in your web scraping toolkit. It allows you to see the building blocks of a website, understand how its elements are nested, and identify the exact pieces of data you need to extract.

## Accessing the Inspector in Google Chrome

Accessing the Chrome Inspector is straightforward. Here's how you can dive into this powerful tool:

1. **Open Google Chrome**: Make sure you have Google Chrome installed on your computer. If not, you can download it from the official website.
2. **Navigate to a Web Page**: Open a web page that you are interested in scraping. This could be any page, perhaps one that lists products, articles, or any data you wish to extract.
3. **Accessing the Inspector**:
   - **Right-Click Method**: Right-click on an element of the webpage you are curious about, such as a piece of text, an image, or a section. In the context menu that appears, select "Inspect." This action opens the Chrome Inspector and highlights the element's HTML in the Elements panel.
   - **Keyboard Shortcut**: Alternatively, you can use a keyboard shortcut to open the Inspector. On Windows and Linux, press `Ctrl+Shift+I`. On macOS, use `Cmd+Opt+I`.
4. **Exploring the Interface**: Once you open the Inspector, you'll see a split screen with the website on one side and the Inspector panel on the other. This panel is divided into various tabs like Elements, Console, Sources, Network, etc., each providing different functionalities.
5. **Elements Tab**: The Elements tab is often the most used for web scraping. It shows the HTML structure of the page and the CSS styles applied to each element. As you hover over different parts of the HTML code in the Elements tab, corresponding parts on the web page are highlighted, helping you understand how the code translates to the visual layout.

The Chrome Inspector is not just a tool; it's a companion in your web scraping journey. As you become more familiar with it, you'll find that it simplifies the process of identifying the right selectors for your scraping scripts, testing XPath or CSS queries, and even debugging issues that arise during scraping.

In the next sections, we'll delve deeper into the functionalities of the Chrome Inspector, exploring how each feature can be leveraged to enhance your web scraping skills. So, let's roll up our sleeves and begin our journey into the heart of web page structures and dynamics!

## Understanding the Elements Panel

As we journey deeper into the realm of web scraping, the Elements Panel in Chrome Inspector emerges as a vital tool. It's like a map of a treasure island, revealing the structure and composition of a webpage. This section will guide you through navigating the DOM (Document Object Model) Tree, inspecting and selecting elements, and understanding the intricacies of HTML and CSS structures.

### Navigating the DOM Tree

The DOM Tree is a hierarchical representation of the structure of a webpage. It's where the HTML of the page comes alive, showing how different elements are nested and related to each other. Here's how to navigate it:

1. **Understanding the Hierarchy**: In the DOM Tree, each line represents an HTML element, like a tag (`<div>`, `<span>`, `<a>`, etc.). These elements are nested, indicating parent-child relationships. Understanding this hierarchy is crucial for effective scraping, as it helps identify the path to the data you need.
2. **Expanding and Collapsing Elements**: Click the small arrow next to an element in the DOM Tree to expand or collapse it. This action reveals or hides its child elements, helping you drill down to the specific part of the page you're interested in.
3. **Highlighting Elements**: As you hover over elements in the DOM Tree, the corresponding section on the webpage will be highlighted. This visual cue is invaluable in understanding how the HTML structure translates to the visual layout.

### Inspecting and Selecting Elements

Inspecting elements is akin to using a magnifying glass to examine the finer details of a webpage:

1. **Selecting Elements**: You can select any element on a webpage directly from the Chrome Inspector. Use the "Select an element in the page to inspect it" tool (the small cursor icon in the top-left corner of the Inspector), then click on the element on the webpage. The DOM Tree will automatically highlight the corresponding HTML.

2. **Contextual Information**: When you select an element, the Elements Panel not only shows the HTML but also provides information about its CSS styles, box model metrics (padding, margin, border), and more.
3. **Editing HTML and CSS**: One of the powerful features of the Chrome Inspector is the ability to modify HTML and CSS on-the-fly. Click on any part of the HTML or CSS in the Elements Panel, and you can start editing. This feature is incredibly useful for testing and seeing immediate visual feedback.

## Understanding HTML and CSS Structures

To master web scraping, a basic understanding of HTML and CSS is essential:

1. **HTML Basics**: HTML is the backbone of web pages, consisting of elements represented by tags. Familiarize yourself with common tags like `<div>`, `<span>`, `<a>`, `<p>`, and their attributes like `class`, `id`, `href`.
2. **CSS and Styling**: CSS defines the style of HTML elements. In the Elements Panel, you can see the CSS styles applied to each selected element. Understanding these styles helps in identifying unique selectors for scraping.
3. **Classes and IDs**: Pay attention to `class` and `id` attributes. They are often used to style and identify specific elements on a webpage, making them crucial for writing precise and efficient scraping scripts.

## Network Analysis for Scraping

Diving into the world of web scraping, one quickly realizes that the secrets of data extraction often lie beneath the surface. This is where the Network Panel of the Chrome Inspector becomes an indispensable ally. This section focuses on harnessing the power of network analysis for scraping, including monitoring network activity, analyzing HTTP requests and responses, and identifying data endpoints.

## Monitoring Network Activity

The Network Panel is like the radar of your scraping vessel, tracking every request and response that happens when a webpage loads or interacts with the server.

1. **Accessing Network Activity**: Open the Network Panel in Chrome Inspector by clicking on the "Network" tab. Once there, reload the webpage to see a list of every network request made by the page.
2. **Understanding the Timeline**: Each request in the Network Panel is accompanied by a timeline. This timeline shows when the request was made, how long it took, and when the response was received. Monitoring this can help you understand the loading behavior of the webpage.
3. **Filtering Requests**: The Network Panel allows you to filter requests by type (like XHR, JS, CSS, Img). For web scraping, XHR (XMLHttpRequest) is often the most relevant, as it pertains to requests made by scripts on the page, often fetching the data you want to scrape.

## Analyzing HTTP Requests and Responses

Each network request and response holds valuable information that can be used for scraping.

1. **Inspecting Details**: Click on any request in the Network Panel to view its details, including the request headers, response headers, preview of the response body, and the response body itself.
2. **Headers**: Request headers contain information about the request, like the User-Agent, Accept-Language, and Cookies. Response headers will tell you about the server's response, including content type and server information. Understanding these headers is crucial for replicating requests programmatically during scraping.
3. **Response Body**: This is where you can see the data returned by the server. For scraping, the response body is often where you'll find the data you want to extract, especially in APIs or AJAX-loaded content.

## Identifying Data Endpoints

One of the key uses of network analysis in scraping is identifying endpoints from which data is loaded.

1. **Finding API Endpoints**: Many modern websites load data dynamically using APIs. These endpoints can often be found in the XHR requests in the Network Panel. Identifying these endpoints can allow you to scrape data directly from the source, which is often more efficient and reliable.
2. **Parameters and Payloads**: Inspect the parameters or payloads of network requests to understand how data is requested. Replicating these in your scraping scripts can allow you to fetch data programmatically.
3. **Response Formats**: Pay attention to the format of the response (JSON, XML, HTML, etc.). This will dictate how you parse and extract the data in your scraping script.

Network analysis is a critical skill in the repertoire of a web scraper. By mastering how to monitor network activity, analyze requests and responses, and identify data endpoints, you are unlocking a more efficient and powerful way to scrape data. This method often leads to more robust and maintainable scraping scripts, as it targets the data at its source, free from the complexities of the page's frontend structure.